PIRATES!

SINK OR SWIM WITH

PIRATE SHIPS

Liam O'Donnell

capstone

© 2018 Heinemann-Raintree
an imprint of Capstone Global Library, LLC
Chicago, Illinois

To contact Capstone Global Library please call 800-747-4992, or visit our web site
www.mycapstone.com

Library of Congress
Cataloging-in-Publication data is available on the Library of Congress website.

ISBN 978-1-4109-8704-4 (library binding)
ISBN 978-1-4109-8708-2 (paperback)
ISBN 978-1-4109-8720-4 (eBook PDF)

Summary
Fast ships, big ships, they could be anywhere in the sea, waiting. Read this book to learn more about pirate
ships and what it took to take care of them.

Editorial Credits
Bradley Cole, editor; Kayla Dohmen, designer; Wanda Winch, media researcher,
Katy LaVigne, production specialist

Photo Credits
We would like to thank the following for permission to reproduce photographs: Alamy Stock Photo: Chronicle,
17, Mary Evans Picture Library, 11; Bridgeman Images: © Look and Learn/Private Collection/Peter Jackson, 9,
Peter Newark Historical Pictures/Private Collection/Charles Murray Padday, 5, Service Historique de la Marine,
Vincennes, France/French School, 27. UIG/Universal History Archive, 13; Getty Images Inc: Bettmann, 29;
iStockphoto: cosmin4000, cover (flag pole), gremlin, 23; National Geographic Creative: Jean-Leon Huens, 25;
Shutterstock: Andrea Izzotti, 21, Andrey_Kuzmin, 2–3 background, Antony McAulay, 22, Arthur Eugene Preston,
15, Elenarts, 19, ilolab, vintage paper texture, Irina Kovancova, cover (bottom right), James Steidl, 7, Kostyantyn
Ivanyshen, cover (bottom left), Molodec, maps, Nik Merkulov, grunge background, pingebat, pirate icons,
sharpner, map directions to island treasure, SoRad, cover (flag), Triff, cover (background), nautical background, TyBy, cover (banner)

Printed and bound in China.
004627

TABLE OF CONTENTS

Some words are shown in bold, **like this**. You can find out what they mean by looking in the glossary.

Pirates

Pirates loved being at sea. Their ship was a place to call home. They made sure the ship was clean and in good shape for sailing the high seas.

Fact

Pirates searched the seas for **merchant ships** to attack and rob. They stole gold, jewels, silks, spices — and sometimes food!

5

Traveling by Ship

During the 1700s, the only way to travel across the sea was in wooden ships. Ships carried people and **cargo** to countries around the world. Cargo often included gold, spices, and jewels.

Pirates tried to rob as many ships as they could. When they found one, they attacked it and took the ship's cargo.

Fact
Pirates often killed anyone who tried to stop them.

Stopping Pirates

Pirates attacked ships that were often filled with gold and goods belonging to certain countries. Pirates cost these countries a lot of money. Many countries sent **navy** ships to stop pirates. Some countries even paid privateers to hunt them down. **Privateers** were men who owned their own ships.

Fact

Francis Drake was a privateer. He worked for Queen Elizabeth I, who ruled England from 1558 to 1603.

Stealing Ships

Sometimes the most valuable treasure from a captured ship was the ship itself. If a pirate captain liked the ship he captured, he often took it for himself.

Fact

Bartholomew Roberts was known as "Black Bart." During his time as a pirate, he captured more than 400 ships.

Pirates were always hunting for faster, stronger, and better-**armed** ships. When a pirate captain kept a captured ship, he would put a trusted crewmember in charge of it. They then sailed together as a group.

Fact

Some pirate captains had as many as 15 ships under their control at a time.

Types of Ships

Each pirate had a favorite type of ship. Some pirates liked small, fast ships that could sneak up on other ships and make quick getaways.

Schooners were small, narrow ships with two tall **masts**. Schooners could sail in very **shallow** water. They could sail between islands where large navy ships couldn't find them.

Fact
Most schooners carried about 75 pirates and 8 cannons.

Sloops were small, fast, and easy to **steer**. A long pole stretched out from the front of a sloop. This was called a bowsprit. Sails along the bowsprit gave the sloop extra speed.

Fact

The more sails a ship had, the faster it moved across the water. Some ships had as many as 20 sails.

Other pirates showed
their strength by
sailing large ships
with many cannons.
Big, square-rigger
ships were harder to
steer than schooners.
But pirates liked them
because their large
size scared many
merchant ship **crews**.

Fact

Square-riggers had up to three
masts. They carried 200 pirates
and had 20 or more cannons.

Ship Weapons

Well-armed ships helped pirates win many of their battles. Pirates often added extra cannons and guns. The cannons poked out of holes called gunports. Cannons fired cannon balls and **grape shot** that caused lots of damage to enemy ships.

Fact

Some merchant ships had fake gunports marked on their sides. The captains hoped the false gunports would fool pirates into thinking their ships were heavily armed.

Looking After Ships

Pirates treated other sailors badly, but they treated their ships with care. They worked hard to keep their ships clean and **seaworthy**. They knew it was the only thing keeping them alive at sea.

Fact

Sailors called their ships "she," not "it." Some people think this custom began because sailors loved their ships as much as their own mothers.

Life at sea could be dangerous. Powerful storms could damage ships. Sometimes sharp rocks could damage the underside of a ship. Pirates continually worked to fix leaks, replace rotten boards, and mend sails. They even scraped **barnacles** off the outside of the ship.

Fact

The boatswain was responsible for making sure that the ship was in good shape each day.

When a ship needed repairs, it had to be turned on its side. This was called **careening**. Pirates had to find safe places to careen their ships. It was dangerous because it left pirates helpless if pirate hunters found them.

Fact

Carpenters were the men who repaired the ship. They might use small pieces of wood to plug any leaks, for example.

A Pirate's Life

Pirates worked hard to keep their ships seaworthy. Their lives could be hard and dangerous. But they knew that their ships were their homes. Strong ships gave pirates the freedom to live as they wanted.

Fact

Blackbeard's ship, the *Queen Anne's Revenge*, had nearly 40 cannons! It weighed 200 tons, making it one of the largest pirate ships ever.

GLOSSARY

armed carrying weapons

barnacles small shellfish that are covered in very hard shells. They attach themselves to the sides of ships.

cargo goods carried by a ship from one country to another

careen to cause a boat to lean or tilt over on one side for cleaning or repairing

carpenter someone who works with wood

crew group of people who work on a ship

grape shot small metal balls that were shot from cannons

mast tall post on a ship to which sails are attached

merchant ship ship carrying items to sell

navy part of the armed services of a country that fights at sea, not on land

privateer sailor who is given permission by a government or other ruler to attack other ships

seaworthy when a ship is able to safely carry people or goods across the sea

shallow area where water is not very deep

steer guide or control the way a ship moves

READ MORE

Books

Lock, Deborah. *Pirates*. Eyewonder. New York, NY: DK Publishing, 2015.

Platt, Richard. *Pirate Diary*. Diary Histories. Cambridge, MA: Candlewick Press, 2014.

Vonne, Mira. *Gross Facts About Pirates*. Gross History. North Mankato, MN: Capstone Press, 2017.

Internet Sites

Use FactHound to find Internet sites related to this book.:

Visit *www.facthound.com*

Just type in 9781410987044 and go.

Check out projects, games and lots more at
www.capstonekids.com

INDEX